God's Redeeming Grace

Through God's Love Victory is Won

SHEILA O'DANIEL

Copyright © 2023 Sheila O'Daniel
All cover art copyright © 2023 Sheila O'Daniel
All Rights Reserved

No part of this book may be reproduced or transmitted in any form or by any means, electronic or mechanical, including photocopying, recording, or by any information storage and retrieval system, without permission in writing from the author.

Publishing Coordinator—Sharon Kizziah-Holmes

Paperback-Press
an imprint of A & S Publishing
Paperback Press, LLC
Springfield, Missouri

ISBN -13: 978-1-960499-69-1

TO GOD BE THE GLORY

To my Lord and Savior Jesus Christ,
who never gives up on me as I continue on this journey of life.

To Mike,
my loving husband and encourager.

To our loving children,
Kayla, Tara,
their spouses and our four grandchildren.

In Memory of Diane and Nancy,
mentors, prayer partners and loving friends.

CONTENTS

- To God be the Glory v
- A Note from the Author i
- God's Redeeming Grace 1
- G R A C E 2
  - His Still *Small* Voice 4
  - Reflection of His Love 6
  - Who I Am In Christ 8
  - A Living Testimony 10
- God's Wonder Through Stillness and Praise 13
- S T I L L N E S S & P R A I S E 14
  - Learning to Abide 16
  - Be Still My Soul 18
  - Blessings 20
  - Rainfall 22
  - Rise and Shine 24
  - Reviving the Soul 26
  - Lord of all Creation 28
  - Sing to the Lord 30
  - Wonders of God 32
  - Remembering 34
- God's Power Through Prayer 37
- P R A Y E R 38
  - Prayer of Importance 40
  - We Gather Together 42
  - God's Perfect Plan 44
- God's Faithfulness Through Trials 47
- T R I A L S 48
  - God's Unfailing Love 50
  - Burdens of Life 52
  - Word of the Lord 54
  - Healing Through Brokenness 56
  - Love of Jesus 58
- God's Victory is Won 61
- V I C T O R Y 62
  - God's Truths 64
  - Peace I Give You 66
  - Fear Has No Power 68
  - Face of God 70
  - Stand Firm in the Faith 72
  - Power in His Name 74
  - Bound No More 76
  - Heaven Bound 78
  - About the Author 80

A Note from the Author

Hummingbirds

    Hummingbirds are very fascinating to watch and to photograph. The humming noise that comes from their fast-beating wings gives them their name. I love to call them my heavenly hummingbirds and can spend hours upon hours gazing at these amazing little birds. Did you know they are the smallest migrating bird and the only birds that can fly backwards? There are so many fun facts about these incredible little creatures. Most of all, as I watch them fly and perch on objects that are near me, I am reminded of God's perfect plan that He has for everything He has created. He created the heavens and earth and everything in it. That, my friend, includes you and me, which leads me to the poetry section of this book.

Poetry

    Poetry is often used as an outlet to express one's emotions or feelings. In the Bible, David was a man after God's own heart. He expressed his feelings openly and honestly before the throne of God. He not only cried out to the Lord for answers and relief from his sufferings, but praised the Lord as he went through them. Praise is a wonderful way to worship. I enjoy writing poetry because it gives me permission to be myself and then to allow God to use it to minister to my heart and others, just as He did the writings of David.

Hummingbirds/Poetry

    Why would I combine hummingbirds with my poetry? Well, hummingbirds are very near and dear to me, the same as expressing myself through poetry. God creates each one of us with our own uniqueness. Hummingbirds remind me of that. They may be small, but they can do incredible things. God says nothing is impossible with Him, so when we put our trust in Jesus, we too, can do incredible things through Him. Putting them together reminds me of the wonderful works of

HIS mighty hand; the works He continues to do not only in my life but in the lives of others and through His creation. May you be blessed!

Sheila O'Daniel

GOD'S REDEEMING GRACE

For it is by grace you have been saved, through faith—and this is not from yourselves, it is the gift of God—not by works, so that no one can boast.
~Ephesians 2:8-9

GRACE

God is the creator of life and has a purpose and a plan for each of us. He pursues us with open arms, waiting for us to open the door of our hearts and let Him in. *"Here I am! I stand at the door and knock. If anyone hears my voice and opens the door, I will come in and eat with that person, and they with me."* (Revelation 3:20) What an invitation to spend eternity with Jesus Christ. His grace saves! *"For it is by grace you have been saved, through faith—and this is not from yourselves, it is the gift of God—not by works, so that no one can boast."* (Ephesians 2:8-9) Life with Jesus is a choice to be made. It's not something we earn, but a gift to freely receive. His grace, His love, His peace and His faithfulness will always be found in a life that is fully committed to the Lord, and once committed, no one can snatch him out of the hand of Jesus. (John 10:28)

With God's grace, we can live a life that has been changed for eternity; we can live each day with an indescribable joy; and we can live in a way that others will see and by faith respond to His love. It doesn't mean life will be perfect by any means, but it does mean with God all things are possible. (Matthew 17:20) Our sins are forgiven...past, present and future. Have you experienced God's redeeming grace? He is so patient, not wanting anyone to perish but everyone to come to Him through repentance. The choice is yours. Join me on this journey of faith and He will provide you with strength to face whatever comes your way today.

HIS STILL SMALL VOICE

The Lord is mighty and powerful.
With understanding no one can fathom,
Yet full of compassions that never fail,
His faithfulness started before Adam.

His still small voice was heard before time,
As Jesus responded in love.
He came down to earth to show us the way,
Obeying God's voice from above.

His bloodshed brought us grace and hope,
And the Holy Spirit to set us apart.
His still small voice is calling out,
"Receive Me into your heart."

He stands at the door and knocks so gently,
Just waiting to be let in.
He will not force Himself upon you,
But waits eagerly to forgive your sin.

Life with Jesus is a choice to be made,
His great love will forever abound.
Peace will come and with it joy,
His faithfulness will always be found.

So, listen to His still small voice,
He's calling out your name.
He'll wash you clean white as snow,
And you'll never be the same.

For Jesus Christ has paid the price,
To set the captives free.
No more chains will hold you down,
And with you, He'll always be.

REFLECTION OF HIS LOVE

The Lord our God is always with us,
And mighty to save is He.
For into this world, He sent His Son,
So we could be set free.

He lived a life, a perfect life,
Yet bore the burdens we bear.
Calling upon His Heavenly Father,
To reveal His loving care.

His Father's love was shown to all,
As He hung there on the Cross.
With a crown of thorns and nail-pierced hands,
To many, He was a loss.

But God the Father had a plan,
Through Jesus Christ His Son.
He bore our sins upon that cross,
And the victory He had won.

But on that cross, it did not end,
Nor in the tomb, you see.
For Christ our Lord did rise again,
As it was meant to be.

The Father's love came forth once more,
The Holy Spirit He did send.
To teach all things to those who believe,
And to help them comprehend.

So when in doubt of your Father's love,
Reflect upon His Word.
There you'll find that love of His,
And your heart will again be stirred.

WHO I AM IN CHRIST

I am a new person in Christ,
An ambassador for His name.
Free from the law of sin and death,
This I do proclaim.

He gives me strength through His glorious power,
Daily as I live.
Knowing there's no condemnation,
And by His blood He does forgive.

A member of a royal priesthood,
And in this world the salt and light.
I was chosen before the creation of the world,
And made perfect in His sight.

I'm assured all things work together for good,
As evil will not prevail.
Hidden with Christ in God alone,
His love will never fail.

Established, anointed, and sealed by God,
I can approach His throne of grace.
Possessing the mind of Jesus Christ,
As each day I do embrace.

Eternally kept in the palm of His hand,
And quickened by His power.
He enables me to always pray,
No matter what the hour.

A visitor in this world am I,
And awaiting for His return.
My destination is heaven bound,
And for this I did nothing to earn.

Being blessed with every spiritual blessing,
The joy that fills the air.
I am a member of God's chosen family,
Wrapped in His loving care.

A Living Testimony

Someday I'll travel home to see,
My Lord and Savior waiting for me.
No more pain and no more tears,
No more sorrow and no more fears.

On streets of gold, I'll walk that day,
With many loved ones along the way.
Peace and joy my heart will rejoice,
Thanking the Lord for my eternal choice.

But on this earth, I am to be,
A living testimony for all to see.
For Jesus Christ has changed my life,
Always at work, removing strife.

Come and hear what God has done,
I'll tell you of the victories won.
A spiritual journey not taken for granted,
For in my heart His Word is planted.

It's by our actions, not words alone,
God's great love is consistently shown.
Others will see, and by faith respond,
Joining God's family with a Christian bond.

Prayer will guide us as we go and share,
Making disciples and showing we care.
God's gentle whispers can always be heard,
Responding to His Spirit and studying His Word.

GOD'S WONDER THROUGH STILLNESS AND PRAISE

Be still and know that I am God; I will be exalted among the nations, I will be exalted in the earth.
~ Psalm 46:10

STILLNESS & PRAISE

Do you long to hear a whisper from God but struggle to be still long enough to listen? If so, you are not alone. In today's society, the struggle is real. In the morning it is so easy to hit the ground running and next thing we know it's time to lay our head on the pillow and rest for the night. We look back and wonder where the day went. I think we have all been there at some point in our journey with the Lord.

For many years now, learning to abide in Christ has been my deepest desire. By taking time to be still and either meditating on His Word or just looking around at the beauty of His creation, my heart has been transformed. Every day God is in the process of revealing more of Himself. His wonders are full of blessings. From the most magnificent mountain ranges to the most beautiful sunrise or sunset and even to the most soothing sounds coming from light rainfall, His wonder fills one's heart with calmness, praise and thankfulness. We experience how powerful yet gentle our Creator is. He cares about every detail of our lives, big or small. When we draw near to the Lord, He draws near to us and will meet us where we are.

When we take a few moments to step away from the routine of the day and be still, God will give us a renewed strength that can only come from Him. He will calm the anxiousness and wipe away the fog so we can see more clearly, through His eyes, the wonders of every season of life. Seasons come and go, but our God never changes. What a blessing!

LEARNING TO ABIDE

Early in the morning I rise,
To meet with my Lord.
Only to be distracted,
And to Him I have ignored.

My heart longs to seek Him,
And draw near to Him each day.
But many times I lack self-discipline,
And go my separate way.

Asking His forgiveness,
And cleansing of my heart.
He knows my deepest desire,
And gives me a fresh new start.

For His will, I do pray,
And carry on as best I know.
Stopping to give thanks and praise,
To Him who loves me so.

He takes my hand and guides me through,
The struggles as they come.
Teaching me to abide in Him,
And to His Word I must succumb.

The joy of knowing my Lord and Savior,
Comes deep within my soul.
He is my hope and driving force,
As to Him I relinquish control.

These words I hum "I Surrender All,"
As I'm reminded of God's grace.
Thanking Him at the end of the day,
For His loving embrace.

BE STILL MY SOUL

Be still my soul and listen well,
For the Lord does want to speak.
He will not grow tired or even weary,
And will strengthen those who are weak.

Be still my soul, for He is God,
The Lord does truly care.
He holds me in the palm of His hand,
And hears my every prayer.

Be still my soul and look to His word,
For the Lord does meet your needs.
He knows my wants and all my desires,
And will guide me as He leads.

Be still my soul and bless His name,
For His beauty, my eyes do see.
You have set Your glory above the heaven,
And upon the earth, You came to be.

Be still my soul and offer praise,
For the wonders of His hand.
My Jesus Christ will someday return,
Revealing the things He has planned.

Be still my soul and remember well,
The Lord is always with you.
Keep looking to Him as you live each day,
And He will see you through.

Blessings

Blessed am I this very day,
As the Lord I seek to serve.
Knowing that His love for me,
Is nothing I deserve.

His blessings come in many ways,
I have to say it's so.
For no matter how I'm feeling,
They always seem to flow.

Driving in the morning hours,
The sun rising as it may.
I see the beauty of God's creation,
In a completely different way.

With the warmth of His Presence,
And the beauty all around.
It causes me to praise Him,
For a blessing I have found.

As the day continues on,
And I'm reminded of His love.
My heart is overwhelmed,
By the blessings from above.

Sitting quietly on the porch,
I try hard to comprehend.
"Why so many blessings, Lord?
And they simply have no end?"

His Spirit speaks so softly,
And gently through the breeze.
Leaving me in awe,
And worshipping Him with ease.

As the night air cools,
And the moon begins to glow.
I look up to the heavens,
And this I truly know.

To my Creator, I'm so thankful,
How He's opened up my eyes.
Seeing answers to my prayers,
Which were blessings in disguise.

For my God knows all things,
And serving Him as I may.
The blessings will keep coming,
As I trust Him and obey.

Rainfall

The sound of steady rainfall,
Brings stillness to my heart.
Reminding me of God's great love,
An awesome way for the day to start.

Be still and know that I am God,
His Word does tell me so.
And I will show you mighty things,
Hidden things you do not know.

I close my eyes and think of Him,
The tenderness of His voice.
Peace and calm does fill my soul,
With praise I sing and rejoice.

"Amazing Grace, how sweet the sound,
That saved a wretch like me.
I once was lost, but now am found,
Was blind, but now I see."

The sound of steady rainfall,
What awareness it does bring.
A reminder of my Lord and Savior,
Who's in control of everything.

RISE AND SHINE

Rise and shine, it's a day to embark,
The light has come and overpowered the dark.
Jesus awaits as we call out His name,
Starting this day to Him, we proclaim.

Great is our Lord and mighty to save,
He sits by our side and makes us brave.
Removing all fear and doubt from within,
My Jesus, He came to take away sin.

His voice is clear, as the Bible we read,
For the Spirit does speak and fulfills our need.
His peace and comfort surrounds my soul,
My Jesus, my Friend, He makes me whole.

His power and majesty, reign from above,
Showering us daily with His true love.
The voice of the Lord will be heard this day,
So rise and seek Him and follow His way.

When the evening does come, remember to say,
"Great is Your faithfulness," to You, I do pray.

Reviving the Soul

Spring has sprung it has indeed,
God's beauty abounds with each new seed.

The wind does blow and the chimes do sound,
Birds fill the air with loud chirps all around.

Beautiful colors all shimmering in the sun,
A smile it brings because of what God has done.

Creator of the heavens and the earth is He,
His mighty hand at work, I know you'll agree.

His splendor and majesty before us are set,
A reminder of why we need never to fret.

For peace He does give us a peace from within,
To live each moment as with God we have been.

Reviving the soul, yes, the Lord does it well,
Through each new seed, His creation does tell.

Lord of all Creation

The Lord of all creation, how majestic is your name!
With my hope in Jesus Christ, I will never be the same.
I lift my eyes up to the hills. Where does my help come from?
To the Lord of all creation, my troubles I overcome.

The rising of the morning sun,
To the Lord I sing aloud.
For He watches over me day and night,
Even through the hazy clouds.
He will not let me fall away,
As many times I fail.
Instead, He takes me by the hand,
And together we walk the trail.
Through the darkest times He is always near,
Never leaving my side.
For He knows the plans that lie ahead,
I trust Him to be my guide.

The Lord of all creation, how majestic is your name!
With my hope in Jesus Christ, I will never be the same.
I lift my eyes up to the hills. Where does my help come from?
To the Lord of all creation, my troubles I overcome.

The setting of the evening sun,
To the Lord, I sing once more.
Lifting my hands, I praise your name,
For the strength to continue to soar.
You never grow tired or weary indeed,
An everlasting God are you.
I put my trust in you alone,
And you see me through and through.
My heart overflows with joy and thanksgiving,
As to you, I lift my voice.
Thank you, Lord God, for your mercy and grace,
And for always giving me a choice.

The Lord of all creation, how majestic is your name!
With my hope in Jesus Christ, I will never be the same.
I lift my eyes up to the hills. Where does my help come from?
To the Lord of all creation, my troubles I overcome.

SING TO THE LORD

Sing to the Lord a new song,
Praise His name all the earth.
Sing to the Lord a new song,
Praise His name for Jesus' birth.

Worship the Lord in spirit and in truth,
Praising His holy name.
Worship the Lord in spirit and in truth,
Praising the One who came.

Honor the King of the most holy One,
Glorifying His Son from above.
Honor the King of the most holy One,
Glorifying His Son for His love.

To our Lord and King who reigns forever,
We honor and worship and sing,
Praising and glorifying Your name on high,
What joy Your love does bring!

Not only joy, but peace and hope,
Our lives are abundantly blessed.
Thank you, Lord Jesus, for your great love,
And in your truth, may we continue to rest.

Wonders of God

Praise the Lord from the heavens,
Praise Him from the heights above.
Praise Him from His sanctuary,
Praise Him for His acts of love.

Sing to the Lord a new song,
Sing to the Lord, all the earth.
Sing to the Lord and praise His name,
Sing to Him for all its worth.

Shout for joy to God our strength,
Shout for joy and clap your hands.
Shout for joy to all creation,
Shout to Him for His great plans.

Awesome wonders God has done,
His wonders will never cease.
Creating praise and song and joy,
My heart overflows with peace.

REMEMBERING

The birds all around sing loud and strong,
While the sun rises high above.
The calmness of the wind brings peace,
To the Lord, my thoughts take hold of.

The sweetness of His still small voice,
How majestic it does sound.
Recalling that He's always near,
With love and kindness that abound.

Reminded of His Word so true,
The many promises He did make.
And knowing deep down in my soul,
Not one of them will He break.

Strength He gives us day by day,
Through Christ, His plan was made.
Reminding me of His faithfulness,
We have nothing to be afraid.

He's coming back! That's what He says,
We're told throughout His Word.
He's coming back for all to see,
Oh how my heart is stirred!

Stand strong and firm as you rest in Him,
Let not your thoughts be swayed.
The Lord Almighty reigns on high,
And hears what you have prayed.

The quietness of this time may end,
But God remains the same.
Throughout this day be reminded of,
The power of His great name.

God's Power Through Prayer

Rejoice always, pray continually, give thanks in all circumstances; for this is God's will for you in Christ Jesus.
~1 Thessalonians 5:16-18

PRAYER

What is your mindset when you approach the throne of God? The Bible says we are to approach His throne boldly and with confidence so we may receive mercy and find grace to help us in our time of need. Prayer is two-way communication with our Heavenly Father; we not only talk, but we also listen. Approaching His throne with worship, praise and thanksgiving prepares the heart to listen more.

Something happens when we pray. Many times I wonder if that is why the Bible says..."Pray without ceasing." (1 Thessalonians 5:16) Whether we pray alone or gather together with other believers, God's ears are attentive to our heartfelt prayers. He longs to hear about our troubles and the desires of our hearts; He delights in hearing our praise and worship and He calls us to intercede on behalf of others. He is a God of wonder and a God of hope.

Through prayer our faith grows. Our minds cannot fathom God's understanding; His ways or His thoughts, but praying in accordance to His will releases His power to accomplish far beyond what we could ever hope or imagine. Where are you in your prayer life? Is prayer your lifeline only when needs arise or is it freely talking to God and daily seeking Him to lead and guide your every step? The throne of God is available to all who call on Him.

Prayer of Importance

Come, let us bow down and worship the Lord,
Let us kneel before His throne.
For He is our God and we are His people,
Who He's never left alone.

"Pray without ceasing," the Lord does say,
"For I hear your mighty cry.
The heavens will tremble and the earth will shake,
As My name is lifted on high.

For when My people who are called by My name,
Humble themselves and pray.
I will hear from heaven and forgive their sins,
Wiping them all away.

My eyes will be open, My ears will be attentive,
To hear every word that is spoken.
Moving in ways that cannot be seen,
While healing a land that is broken.

Keep always rejoicing and continue in prayer,
For My promises I wrote long ago.
Bring comfort and peace and joy to the heart,
As life's trials will continue to grow."

Give thanks to the Lord for He is good,
His love will forever endure.
Give thanks to the Lord and praise His name,
For in Christ you're forever secure.

WE GATHER TOGETHER

We gather together, in one accord,
Seeking to hear a word from the Lord.
We bow and ask You to show us the way,
To lead and guide us as we pray.

We humble ourselves, and lift up our hands,
Asking, You Lord, to please heal our land.
Your Word stands true as we watch and we wait,
Open the heavens, open the gates.

Pour out your Spirit, for we praise your name.
Prepare our hearts, Your Word we proclaim.
The heavens open and Your light does shine,
A reminder sent; all will be fine.

Your Presence brings warmth and comfort and peace,
Causing our faith to further increase.
It is not by sight that we live each day,
But trusting Your truths and what they say.

The works of Your hand we've seen them before,
Through nature and sickness and much more.
We call upon You, Your power and grace,
Teach us Your will, Your Word we embrace.

We repent and turn from our wicked ways,
Giving You thanks, and giving You praise.
A God of wonder, and a God of hope,
A God of great strength who helps us cope.

We gather together in one accord,
Knowing great things, will come from our Lord.
His plan is unfolding before our eyes,
We thank you Lord for hearing our cries.

God's Perfect Plan

The Word of the Lord is right and true,
As He watches over both me and you.
His faithfulness will be our shield,
As to His will we continue to yield.

Our faith is seen when we rest in Him,
Even at times when things look grim.
Enduring such moments we know we're blest,
For in God's great love is where we rest.

Such delight in us the Lord does take,
In Him we know there's never a mistake.
He delights and quiets us with His love,
And rejoices with singing that comes from above.

God's plan unfolds as we live each day,
A hope and a future He gives as we pray.
Calling upon Him our hearts will soon find,
Our God is there waiting for all of mankind.

His plan is perfect and in faith we do live,
Trusting our God as strength He does give.
Moment by moment, and day by day,
We surrender it all, as He shows us the way.

God's Faithfulness Through Trials

And the God of all grace, who called you to his eternal glory in Christ, after you have suffered a little while, will himself restore you and make you strong, firm and steadfast.
~1 Peter 5:10

TRIALS

When someone becomes a believer it doesn't mean they are exempt from experiencing tough times. For the Bible says we are to consider it pure joy whenever we face trials of many kinds because the testing of our faith produces perseverance and perseverance must finish its work so that we may be mature and complete, not lacking anything. (James 1:2-4) It says **whenever** we face trials, not *if* we face trials. So, we must realize trials will come.

Through our brokenness, God creates beauty. Are you going through some really hard times right now? Sometimes it's difficult to see or understand why things happen while we are in the midst of them but God's faithfulness is always present. He takes our failures, our fears, our anxiousness, our mourning, our anger, our bitterness, our unforgiveness, our health issues, and the many more things we may struggle with and works them out for our good and His glory. In His faithfulness He keeps His promises.

He is close to the brokenhearted and brings healing through the pain. He walks through the storms of life with us and will never leave us alone. God's faithfulness never ends.

No one likes to go through tough times, but without them how can our faith grow? When we take the hand of Jesus and walk through them, He will give us peace, a peace that transcends all understanding. He is faithful to do it.

GOD'S UNFAILING LOVE

My heart is broken and life seems hopeless,
All dreams have come and gone.
I look to the heavens where my help does come,
To the Maker I am drawn.

My Shepherd, my Rock, the Lord of my life,
My Shield, my Strength, my Stronghold.
I call to the Lord who is worthy of praise,
As my heart just seems to grow cold.

I cry for help and He hears my voice,
His hand reaches out for mine.
Help me, oh Lord, out of the pit of despair,
And lead me back to Thine.

The cords of death, they entangle me,
Causing darkness to appear.
I cling to your hand, holding it tight,
Slowly the darkness begins to clear.

You reached down from on high and rescued me,
Lifting me out of the pit.
Your strength and power destroyed my enemy,
Encouraging me not to quit.

My God does hold me tight and secure,
In the palm of His hand I belong.
His ways are perfect, flawless and good,
My faith is growing strong.

I sing praises to God for His unfailing love,
His faithfulness stands true.
The trials of life will continue to come,
But with God He'll see me through.

BURDENS OF LIFE

My heart is ever longing,
For the word of the Lord to speak.
For no good thing will be withheld,
From those in Him do seek.

The burdens of this life will come,
But they're not to weigh us down.
For the yoke of the Lord is easy,
By enduring we'll receive a crown.

Be still before the Lord He says,
And patiently wait on Me.
May your heart be ever strengthened,
As in prayer with bended knee.

The time will come I believe it so,
God's faithfulness stands strong.
His eternal glory will forever shine,
As to Him our burdens belong.

With an outstretched hand He cares for us,
And mighty to save is He.
For someday soon He will return,
From the burdens we'll be set free.

The word of God did speak once more,
And until that day does come.
He'll roll the burdens of my heart away,
And to them I'll not succumb.

WORD OF THE LORD

The Lord is close to the brokenhearted,
His Word is right and true.
For those who are crushed in spirit He saves,
And gives comfort through and through.

I sought the Lord, and He answered me,
His Word is the only way.
Delivering me from all my fears,
To Him I continue to pray.

Taste and see that the Lord is good,
His Word is full of life.
Blessed is the one who takes refuge in Him,
For God will remove all the strife.

Those who look to the Lord are radiant,
His Word is moved with light.
Their faces are never covered with shame,
As with sin they continue to fight.

The Lord redeems His servants with care,
His Word is mighty and strong.
None are condemned who take refuge in Him,
As this journey we travel along.

Exalt the Lord at all times we will do,
His Word is so pure and sweet.
His Praise will always be upon my lips,
As someday the Lord I will meet.

HEALING THROUGH BROKENNESS

Through brokenness comes healing,
And through healing will come peace.
While mending broken hearts,
God's love will never cease.

When your heart is grieving,
And sorrow fills your soul.
Lift your hands up to the Lord,
And give Him all control.

Honesty is what God wants,
As your feelings you let go.
For grieving is a process,
And helps your faith to grow.

Through brokenness comes healing,
And through healing will come hope.
While mending broken hearts,
God's love will help you cope.

The pain is real I know it's so,
Each breath is hard to take.
But Jesus Christ, He understands,
And will heal the worst heartache.

Humbly cry out unto the Lord,
He'll guide and counsel you.
For pain is never wasted,
In God's Kingdom He foreknew.

Through brokenness comes healing,
And through healing will come joy.
While mending broken hearts,
God's love will He employ.

LOVE OF JESUS

Taking the hand of Jesus,
And walking through this day.
My eyes are opened more and more,
As I watch Him lead the way.

Walking along this path together,
I can see His love so sweet.
Caring for the needs of others,
His ways are such a treat.

Forgiveness in His eyes shine bright,
For man that scorned Him so.
He looks to me and says so softly,
"Come on my child, let's go."

I follow Him with hand in hand,
And a big smile on His face,
I notice the pure joy flowing out,
With everyone He does embrace.

No matter if they believe in Him,
Or go their separate way.
His heart of true forgiveness,
Continues throughout the day.

When evening comes, He speaks once more,
As He looks within my eyes,
"Follow My example daily.
Don't let unforgiveness arise."

The love of Jesus, how freely it flows,
Upon everyone around.
Take His hand and follow Him,
His love through you will abound.

God's Victory is Won

Finally, be strong in the Lord and in his mighty power. Put on the full armor of God, so that you can take your stand against the devil's schemes.
~Ephesians 6:10-11

VICTORY

Spiritual battles wage war within us every day. Jesus came to give life and give it abundantly but the devil prowls around like a lion seeking to devour that which God has created. So how do you respond when entering a battle? For many it's the battle of the mind. It's our own thinking that can drag us down causing loneliness, depression, fear, despair and even hopelessness. When we listen to the lies of the enemy, we will start to feel defeated and useless.

With Jesus there is hope! When we submit to the Lord the devil has to flee. While Jesus was tempted in the wilderness, He defeated the devil by using the Word of God, which is the sword of the Spirit as mentioned in Ephesians 6:17. He replaced the lies with God's truths and overcame the enemy. What a great example for us as Christians. God has given us all we need to stand firm. We have the full armor of God and we have the same power living in us that raised Jesus from the dead. We can stand firm against the ways of the enemy, who is seeking to devour us.

God's mighty power has already won the victory. Through faith in Christ we also have won the victory. So let us resist the devil by standing firm in the faith, putting on the full armor and walking in the power of His strength.

God's Truths

Do you tremble at the sound,
Of the enemy's voice?
Whispering lies that may cause you,
To make the wrong choice?

Prowling around like a lion, the devil does seek,
To devour your soul or to make you feel weak.
Believing his lies will bring fear and much pain,
With times of discouragement and with nothing to gain.

No peace will you find, no comfort will you feel,
Lost in destruction the lies will seem real.
In a pit of despair your mind is not clear,
Your body is trembling and full of much fear.

But the lies can be silenced with one single name,
Jesus Christ the Good Shepherd removes all our shame.
Hope He does give us with peace and much love,
But you must resist the devil with this name from above.

Draw near to the Lord and submit to His ways,
The devil will flee, to the Lord you will praise.
The trembling will cease, and the fear will subside,
Whispers of God's promises will then be your guide.

The full armor of God will you take in your hand,
And put it on daily as the Lord fully planned.
The promises He provides will help us succeed,
Standing firm in the faith unshakeable as can be.

The enemy's voice can no longer be heard,
Just whispers of God's love,
From the promises in His Word!

Peace I Give You

This day I live as unto You,
Searching my heart for words that are true.
Not knowing the outcome but living this day,
Trusting my Savior as He leads the way.

Moment by moment I walk in His peace,
By His great love that does not cease.
But the moment my focus is turned away,
Clouds of despair will come to stay.

The enemy of darkness is here to destroy,
Roaming the earth for his plans to employ.
Seeking to devour the children of the Lord,
We must take a stand and fight with the sword.

The Sword of the Spirit is the Word of God,
Alive and powerful and is not flawed.
The more you memorize and hide in your heart,
Your focus on the Lord will not depart.

The peace He gives will forever reside,
Living in you with great joy from inside.
As your focus remains on the truths of His Word,
No room for the enemy's lies will be heard.

Moment by moment may you walk through this day,
Holding to the truths so your heart will not sway.
Trusting the Lord as you live as unto Him,
Allowing His light to never grow dim.

Fear Has No Power

The enemy of fear changes a life,
It makes one anxious and causes much strife.
Tearing apart friendships leaving bitterness and pain,
It makes one lonely with nothing to gain.

Allowing such fear, it takes away peace,
Causing discontentment and joy to cease.
Self-seeking it becomes as it grips a longing soul,
Fear draws one inward taking up control.

It has no power over a child of the King,
God does remind us of this very thing.
Strong and courageous we are to be every day,
For He's with us always leading the way.

He gives us armor and weapons we need,
To fight the fear when it rises, indeed.
His love overrides it and His Word keeps us driven,
For the spirit of fear God never has given.

So, may the peace of Christ rule in your heart,
Melting away fear as soon as it starts.
Standing firm on His Word, the truth will set you free,
In the name of Jesus fear has to flee!

FACE OF GOD

There comes a time when I fall to my knees,
And cry from the depth of my heart.
I call to the Lord who is worthy of praise,
And my tears they soon depart.

For into His face I intently look,
And there before me I do find.
His eyes are fixed on me alone,
So compassionate and kind.

With eyes aglow and holding me tight,
My heart begins to calm.
I'm reminded of His faithfulness,
As it's written in the Psalm.

The earth may tremble or violently shake,
But nothing shall I fear.
For He whispers in His still small voice,
"My child I am near."

I look to Him with joy filled eyes,
With faith I begin to speak.
Praising God who is worthy and true,
And with a humbled heart I do seek.

For God alone is my salvation,
My ever-present help in need.
His comfort draws me to His Word,
As closely I must read.

For into His face I look once more,
A twinkle in His eyes I see.
He's answered prayer again this day,
A special one for me.

Stand Firm in the Faith

The Lord is my strength and my shield,
And to Him I do trust and will yield.
For my heart leaps for joy with songs of His praise,
Giving glory to Him all my days.

He gives strength to the weary and more power to the weak,
He's my refuge and help as to Him I do seek.
With feet like a deer, He enables me to tread,
To tread on the heights, with strength to look ahead.

When my heart seems so troubled and afraid I do feel,
My Jesus gives peace, a peace that is real.
"Do not fear," He does say, "for wherever you go,
I'm with you, I'm with you, for this you must know."

The Lord is my light and my salvation is He,
The stronghold of my life, so the fear has to flee.
I sought the Lord and an answer I did hear,
From my fears I was delivered for my God He was near.

Stand firm, stand firm in the faith you must stand,
For the devil will take you if you lend him your hand.
Be courageous; be strong, for the devil does scheme,
Put on the full armor and let your light gleam.

Therefore, my dear brothers, stand firm as can be,
For freedom Christ came to set us all free.
Stand firm in the faith, be courageous and strong,
Stand firm in the faith, for to Christ you belong.

Power in His Name

The Alpha and Omega, first and the last,
Washes away sin and mistakes from our past.
Wonderful Counselor and mighty to save,
With His great power He rose from the grave.

We call to the Lord, who is worthy of praise,
And through His Word we learn of His ways.
It's God who arms us with strength for each day,
Who reigns down His love and helps guide our way.

My light and my salvation, my counselor and friend,
The Lord Jesus Christ I will always defend.
His ways are perfect, they're right and complete,
Leaving the enemy in a state of defeat.

For when I am afraid I will trust in Thee,
My protector He is and forever will be.
My rock and my fortress, my deliverer, my shield,
The Almighty God to whom I will yield.

There's power in the name of Christ Jesus our King,
Creator and Ruler of everything!
Miraculous signs He performs to this day,
As we call out His name and continue to pray.

The Alpha and Omega, the beginning and end,
At the return of Christ Jesus every knee will bend.
Every tongue will confess and proclaim Him as Lord,
"To God be the glory," we'll declare in one accord.

BOUND NO MORE

Prowling like a lion the devil is he,
Seeking to devour those who are free.
He comes as a thief to kill, steal and destroy,
To bind us in chains and to rob us of joy.

He fills our thoughts with lies upon lies,
And imitates God as if in disguise.
His only desire is to sink us so low,
That our hearts would be hardened,
And depression would grow.

But in the name of JESUS he has to move on,
For God holds the devil in His hand like a pawn.
He has no authority upon those who believe,
Just whispers lies and tries to deceive.

But little does he know the victory has been won,
God will complete what He has begun.
The story is told from Genesis to Revelation,
Jesus Christ reigns over all…over all of creation!

The devil may be heard with a whisper or a shout,
But God's Word is the truth and that we mustn't doubt.
Stand tall and stand proud for God is at work,
Why else would the enemy continue to smirk.

Submit to the Lord then and walk in His ways,
Lift up your voice and sing of His praise.
From the grave Jesus rose to the heavens above,
Sending down the Holy Spirit wrapped in His love.

The victory has been won and no more are we bound,
Live free in the Spirit with peace all around!

HEAVEN BOUND

Heaven bound someday I'll be,
Face to face the Lord I'll see.
On my knees I'll fall to Thee,
Heaven bound someday I'll be.

With angels worshipping around His throne,
My eyes will fix on God alone.
Hearing His voice so soft and sweet,
"Come to Me," I'll run to meet.

Embrace we will with a loving hug,
As tears flow down all safe and snug.
His eyes so bright and filled with peace,
I know His love will never cease.

Reminded now on earth I live,
I must continue to freely give.
For God gave up His only Son,
By His blood the victory was won.

Someday soon I'll be heaven bound,
With the love of God flowing all around.
Praising the Lord, what a glorious sound,
Someday soon I'll be heaven bound!

About the Author

Sheila O'Daniel has a love for nature and God's amazing creation. She is a wife, mother and grandmother and enjoys spending time with her family and friends. Much of her time is spent outside. Whether traveling to see her kids and grandchildren, touring the National Parks or just relaxing on the porch, she is always observing the footprints of God. Her heart's desire is to help others find encouragement and hope by using the gifts God has given her.

Made in the USA
Coppell, TX
20 May 2024